CW00588153

A Place to Play

Janet and Allan Ahlberg

Collins

Brick Street School is closed.
The children are on holiday for a week.
This is what the Brick Street Boys do
with their holiday.

On Monday they play football in the street.
They play at passing, heading and shooting,

and hide-and-seek.

But a policeman comes.
"Hello, hello, hello," he says. Then the
policeman tells them to play in the park.

On Tuesday they play football in the
swimming baths.

They play at heading and passing,

and horse-riding.

But an attendant comes. He blows his whistle. "No balls in here," he says, and tells them to go away.

On Wednesday they play football on the bus.

They play at heading.

But the conductor says,
"I'll smack your bottoms good and hard."

The driver says, "Get off my bus."

On Thursday it rains.

On Friday they play football in the supermarket.

They play at passing

and shooting,

and motor-racing.

But the manager comes.
"Dear me, dear me," he says,
and he asks them to go and play in the park.

On Saturday they play football in the park.

They play at shooting, heading and passing,

and cowboys-and-Indians.

But the park keeper comes.
"I'm not having this," he says,
"this is a respectable park."
He tells them to go home.

On Sunday the Brick Street Boys stay in bed.

The next day the school is open again
and the holiday is over.

The Brick Street Boys play football
in the playground.

They tell jokes to Mr Mott and drink pop at

half-time and are glad to be back.

Other books about the Brick Street Boys:

Here are the Brick Street Boys
Sam the Referee
Fred's Dream
The Great Marathon Football Match

First published 1975
This edition 1986
© Janet and Allan Ahlberg 1975

ISBN 0 00 138015-X

All rights reserved. No part of this
publication may be reproduced, stored
in a retrieval system, or transmitted,
in any form or by any means, electronic,
mechanical, photocopying, recording or
otherwise, without the prior permission
of William Collins Sons & Co Ltd,
8 Grafton Street, LONDON W1X 3LA.

Printed in Italy by New Interlitho, Milan